ARTIFICIAL INTELLIGENCE DEMYSTIFIED: WHAT EVERYONE SHOULD KNOW

A Plain-English Introduction to AI
and Its Impact on Society

 www.reallygreatsite.com Hello@reallygreatsite.com

KRIS ERIKSEN

Artificial Intelligence Demystified: What Everyone Should Know

A Plain-English Introduction to AI and Its Impact on Society

This book was professionally typeset on Reedsy.
Find out more at reedsy.com

Contents

1

Chapter 1: Introduction to AI

Artificial Intelligence (AI) is a term that conjures up images of futuristic robots, self-driving cars, and computers that can outsmart the best human minds at chess or trivia. While there is some truth to these ideas, AI in the real world is both more ordinary and more profound than people often realize. Put simply, AI refers to computer systems or machines that can perform tasks typically requiring human intelligence. These tasks may include learning from experience, recognizing patterns, making decisions, or understanding language.

The fundamental goal of AI is to allow machines to exhibit behaviors once thought to be the exclusive domain of humans. For example, when you talk to a virtual assistant like Siri or Alexa, the software is using AI techniques to process the sound of your voice, interpret what you're asking, and deliver a relevant response. Similarly, recommendations you see on streaming services or e-commerce sites come from AI models that analyze your past behavior to predict what you might enjoy or want to purchase next.

However, AI isn't just about convenience and personalization. It also drives innovations in healthcare, finance, education, and many other sectors. It enables faster and more accurate data analysis for doctors diagnosing diseases, or financial experts detecting fraud. In education, AI systems can tailor learning experiences to individual students, offering personalized feedback in real-time. Across industries, companies use AI to optimize processes, reduce costs, and deliver more value to customers.

Despite these benefits, AI also comes with a set of challenges and concerns. Many people worry about job displacement, privacy issues, and bias in automated decision-making. These are legitimate concerns that must be addressed by developers, policymakers, and society as a whole to ensure that AI is used responsibly and for the greater good.

In this book, we aim to demystify AI by breaking down core concepts into plain-English explanations. We will trace its history, exploring how early pioneers laid the groundwork for modern breakthroughs. We will also delve into the technical concepts—like machine learning, deep learning, and neural networks—in an accessible way, without unnecessary jargon. Most importantly, we will discuss the real-world impact of AI, shedding light on ethical considerations, policy-making, and what the future could hold.

By the time you finish reading, you will have a clear sense of what AI is, how it works, and why it matters. You'll also be better equipped to join the ongoing conversation about AI's role in shaping our collective future.

2

Chapter 2: A Brief History of AI

To truly appreciate the current landscape of artificial intelligence, it helps to know where it all started. The idea of creating
machines that can "think" can be traced back centuries in myths,
legends, and works of science fiction. However, modern AI
research began in earnest in the mid-20th century.

One pivotal moment came in 1950 when mathematician and
computer scientist Alan Turing proposed the question, "Can
machines think?" In his famous paper, he introduced what
is now known as the Turing Test: a method for determining
whether a machine's intelligence is indistinguishable from that
of a human. This question sparked discussions that continue to
this day.

The official birth of AI as a field is often dated to the 1956
Dartmouth Conference, organized by John McCarthy, Marvin
Minsky, Nathaniel Rochester, and Claude Shannon. The at-
tendees were optimistic about the potential of machines to
replicate human thought processes. Early research focused

on symbolic AI—teaching computers to manipulate symbols and rules to solve problems. Scientists built programs that could solve algebraic equations or prove logical theorems. While these achievements were impressive for the time, they relied on carefully handcrafted rules and didn't scale well to more complex tasks.

The field experienced its first "AI winter" in the 1970s when progress slowed. Researchers discovered that many real-world problems were too complex for rule-based systems, and funding dried up. However, new techniques and the rise of personal computing led to a resurgence in the 1980s, with "expert systems" that captured the knowledge of specialists in fields such as medicine and finance.

A major breakthrough occurred in the late 1990s. In 1997, IBM's Deep Blue defeated world chess champion Garry Kasparov, proving that computers could outmatch even the best human minds in specific tasks. Yet, general AI—that is, AI that can handle a broad range of tasks like a human—remained elusive. Another lull followed, but the 21st century brought exponential increases in computational power, massive datasets, and new algorithms.

One of the most significant developments was the rise of machine learning and, more specifically, deep learning. Powered by neural networks that take inspiration from the human brain, deep learning algorithms have achieved remarkable results in image recognition, speech processing, and even complex strategy games like Go. Today, AI research spans countless domains, from natural language processing to robotics, and

4

governments and corporations invest heavily in advancing this transformative technology.

This history sets the stage for our modern AI era—an era characterized by rapid growth, evolving challenges, and tremendous potential for reshaping society. The journey from the early days of symbolic AI to the powerful learning systems of today illustrates both the complexity of the field and the creativity required to make machines "intelligent."

3

Chapter 3: Key AI Concepts

Before delving deeper into how AI is applied, it's useful to outline some foundational concepts that underpin the field. While AI might seem like a single technology, it's actually a broad set of techniques, philosophies, and goals aimed at making machines capable of tasks that require intelligence.

1. **Data**: At the heart of modern AI lies data. Whether you're training a language model or a computer vision system, data is essential for teaching the system what to recognize and how to react. The quality and quantity of data often determine how successful an AI application will be.
2. **Algorithms**: These are sets of rules and calculations that machines use to analyze data. In AI, algorithms can adapt and learn patterns, rather than following static, pre-defined instructions. The more advanced the algorithm, the better it can generalize from data and handle new, unseen examples.
3. **Machine Learning**: This is a subset of AI focused on enabling machines to learn from data without being explicitly

programmed. Traditional programming involves giving a computer a detailed list of instructions. Machine learning flips that paradigm: provide the machine with examples and let it find the underlying rules or patterns on its own.

4. **Deep Learning**: A subfield of machine learning, deep learning uses layered structures called neural networks, which are loosely inspired by the human brain. These neural networks can uncover complex patterns in vast amounts of data, making them highly effective for tasks like image recognition, speech synthesis, and language translation.

5. **Neural Networks**: These are the building blocks of deep learning. A neural network consists of layers of interconnected "neurons" that transform input data (such as an image) into meaningful output (like identifying a cat). Each connection has a weight that the network adjusts through a process called backpropagation, improving performance over time.

6. **Reinforcement Learning**: This approach involves training models to make decisions in complex environments. The AI agent interacts with the environment, receives feedback in the form of rewards or penalties, and adjusts its actions accordingly. This technique has been used successfully in robotics and game-playing.

7. **Narrow vs. General AI**: Narrow AI excels at a single task, such as detecting spam in emails or recommending movies. General AI, on the other hand, refers to an AI system that can handle any intellectual task a human can—a level of intelligence that does not yet exist.

Understanding these core concepts is critical for recognizing both the potential and limitations of AI. By grasping how data, algorithms, and models come together, it becomes easier to see how AI can be leveraged responsibly and effectively across countless applications.

4

Chapter 4: Machine Learning

Machine learning is often described as the engine that drives modern AI. In the traditional programming model, you feed data into a set of step-by-step instructions, and the computer follows those instructions to produce an output. In machine learning, this approach is turned on its head. Instead of explicitly telling the computer how to interpret the data, you give it examples and let it find the patterns or "rules" on its own.

This approach is possible thanks to statistical methods that help machines infer relationships between variables in a dataset. For instance, if you have a dataset of houses along with their features (e.g., square footage, number of bedrooms, location) and prices, a machine learning algorithm can learn how these features correlate with the sale price. Once trained, you can feed the model a new house's features, and it will predict its price based on what it learned.

Machine learning can be broadly categorized into three types: supervised, unsupervised, and reinforcement learning.

- **Supervised Learning**: In supervised learning, you provide the algorithm with labeled data. For example, you might supply a set of images labeled "cat" and another set labeled "dog." The algorithm learns what differentiates cats from dogs. When given a new image, it applies its learned understanding to classify the image correctly.

- **Unsupervised Learning**: This involves training the algorithm on unlabeled data. The algorithm seeks patterns, clusters, or structures within the data on its own. An example is grouping customers by purchasing behavior without knowing in advance which categories or groups might exist.

- **Reinforcement Learning**: Here, an AI "agent" interacts with an environment and learns to achieve a goal through trial and error, guided by rewards or penalties. This is how AI systems have learned to play board games (like Go and chess) or navigate mazes.

The power of machine learning lies in its ability to adapt. As you feed it more data, the model refines its understanding of the task, often improving its performance. However, this also means that machine learning models can reflect and even amplify biases present in their training data. If the data is incomplete or skewed, the model's decisions will be likewise flawed. Additionally, machine learning models are typically good at specific tasks but lack the breadth of understanding a human has.

Despite these limitations, machine learning has opened doors in fields as varied as healthcare, finance, retail, and transportation. By learning patterns from vast datasets, machine learning models can detect diseases early, recommend products, flag fraudulent transactions, and even pilot autonomous vehicles— all with minimal human intervention. It is this ability to learn from examples and get better over time that makes machine learning a cornerstone of modern AI.

5

Chapter 5: Deep Learning

While machine learning has proven revolutionary, deep learning takes those breakthroughs a step further by using artificial neural networks structured in multiple layers. These layered networks are what give deep learning its name. Each layer in a neural network transforms the input data in some way—extracting progressively more complex features—until it arrives at an output that represents the network's best guess for a specific task.

Deep learning's power lies in its capacity to automatically discover intricate patterns in data. For instance, in image recognition, the first layer of the network might learn to detect simple edges or corners. A deeper layer might then combine these edges to identify shapes or textures. Finally, an even deeper layer could recognize the combination of shapes as a specific object like a dog, cat, or car. This hierarchical approach to feature extraction means that deep learning models often require less manual feature engineering; instead, they learn to optimize these features through repeated training.

Training a deep neural network, however, can be computationally intensive. Large datasets and powerful hardware—especially graphics processing units (GPUs) and tensor processing units (TPUs)—are crucial to handling the vast number of calculations required. But when done right, the results can be astonishing. Deep learning models have achieved near-human or even superhuman performance in tasks like speech recognition, language translation, game playing, and image classification.

One of the remarkable achievements in deep learning came when DeepMind's AlphaGo defeated the world champion Go player Lee Sedol in 2016. Go is an ancient board game considered more complex than chess, with an enormous number of possible moves. AlphaGo's success was attributed to a combination of deep neural networks and reinforcement learning, underscoring how these advanced techniques can tackle challenges once deemed too complex for computers.

Despite these successes, deep learning also has limitations. Neural networks can be "black boxes" in the sense that it's often difficult to interpret how they arrived at a particular decision. This lack of transparency raises concerns in critical fields like healthcare or finance, where understanding the reasoning behind a decision can be just as important as the decision itself. Additionally, deep learning models are data-hungry and can struggle when data is scarce. They may also inherit biases from their training datasets, leading to unfair or inaccurate outcomes if not carefully managed.

Nonetheless, deep learning remains one of the most promising frontiers in AI. Its ability to learn from unstructured data—such as raw images, audio, or text—opens the door to numerous applications. As research continues to evolve, deep learning will likely remain a pivotal force in driving AI innovation.

6

Chapter 6: Natural Language Processing

Natural Language Processing (NLP) is a branch of AI that focuses on enabling machines to understand, interpret, and generate human language. Language is inherently complex, riddled with nuances such as grammar, context, tone, and cultural references. This complexity makes NLP one of the most challenging yet fascinating areas in AI.

One of the main applications of NLP is text analysis, where algorithms identify patterns or sentiments in large bodies of text. For example, companies might use sentiment analysis tools to gauge public opinion about their brand across social media platforms. On an individual level, email providers often use NLP to filter out spam, scanning messages for keywords or suspicious structures.

Another growing application is in language generation, where systems create coherent text in response to prompts. These range from auto-completion features in your email to more advanced models that can write entire articles or draft legal documents. Chatbots and virtual assistants, such as Apple's Siri, Amazon's Alexa, or Google Assistant, rely heavily on NLP to process spoken language and generate human-like responses.

A subfield known as **neural machine translation** has drastically improved the quality of translations between languages. By using deep learning techniques, translation models can capture contextual nuances far better than earlier rule-based systems. While machine translation isn't perfect, it has become sufficiently accurate to assist businesses in communicating across language barriers and individuals in navigating multilingual content.

One of the key challenges in NLP is ambiguity. Human language is filled with words that have multiple meanings (homonyms), idiomatic expressions, and slang. Discerning context—such as whether "bank" refers to a financial institution or a riverbank— requires complex modeling of both linguistic and situational cues. Advances in deep learning have made these tasks more feasible, with models like the Transformer architecture (used in systems such as BERT or GPT) showing significant improvements in understanding context and producing fluent text.

Ethical concerns also surface in NLP. Large language models trained on expansive datasets might inadvertently learn biases present in the text. They can then reproduce or even amplify these biases, leading to problematic outputs such as hate speech or misinformation if safeguards are not in place. Additionally, NLP raises questions about data privacy, especially when personal communications are analyzed.

Despite these concerns, NLP continues to make strides in improving how humans and computers interact. From real-time translation to voice-activated personal assistants, NLP is transforming the way we communicate with technology, making it more intuitive, responsive, and accessible for people around the globe.

7

Chapter 7: Computer Vision

Computer Vision is the field of AI that enables machines to interpret and understand visual information from the world, such as images, videos, or even live camera feeds. The goal is to replicate—and in some cases surpass—the abilities of the human visual system in detecting, classifying, and interpreting objects and scenes.

One of the fundamental tasks in computer vision is **image recognition**, which involves identifying objects or scenes within an image. For instance, a trained model might look at a photograph and label it as containing a cat, a car, or a tree. Beyond simple labeling, more advanced techniques like **object detection** can locate and draw bounding boxes around each object, while **segmentation** can identify the exact shape of each object within the image.

Deep learning, particularly using convolutional neural networks (CNNs), has dramatically improved the accuracy of these tasks. CNNs apply filters to the image that capture features like edges, corners, or textures. Deeper layers of the network then combine these features to form a high-level understanding of what's in the image. This approach has enabled breakthroughs in facial recognition, medical imaging analysis, and autonomous driving.

Facial recognition, for example, can identify individuals by analyzing unique facial features. This technology is used in security systems, mobile phone unlocking, and even social media platforms to suggest tags for photos. However, facial recognition also raises ethical and privacy concerns, particularly when used without explicit user consent or in surveillance.

In healthcare, computer vision is revolutionizing the way doctors diagnose diseases. AI systems can analyze medical images such as X-rays, MRIs, or CT scans to detect anomalies with remarkable accuracy. Radiologists use these tools to highlight suspicious areas that may indicate cancer or other conditions, improving early detection and patient outcomes.

Autonomous vehicles rely heavily on computer vision to "see" the road, identify other vehicles, pedestrians, and obstacles. Through a combination of cameras, LiDAR, and radar, these vehicles create a real-time map of their surroundings, enabling them to navigate safely. While the technology has not yet achieved perfect reliability, progress is rapid, and many experts believe fully autonomous cars are not too far in the future.

The potential of computer vision extends beyond these examples, touching fields like agriculture (monitoring crop health via aerial imagery), retail (automating checkout processes), and manufacturing (quality control). As camera technology and image processing algorithms continue to advance, computer vision is poised to remain a cornerstone of AI applications, enhancing our ability to interpret the visual world in ways that can benefit industries and society alike.

8

Chapter 8: Robotics and AI

Robotics and AI often go hand in hand, bringing to life the futuristic notion of intelligent machines capable of performing complex, real-world tasks. At its core, a robot is a machine that can sense, think, and act in its environment. When AI algorithms power a robot's "brain," it gains the ability to adapt, learn, and respond more intelligently to changing conditions.

Historically, robots have been used in manufacturing, where they perform repetitive tasks on assembly lines. These industrial robots are typically programmed with fixed routines, requiring significant reprogramming to accommodate any change in the production process. Modern AI techniques are transforming this rigid approach, making robots more flexible and capable of working alongside humans. Collaborative robots, or "cobots," can learn tasks by demonstration, detect human presence to avoid accidents, and adapt to variations in the production line.

Another area of robotics greatly benefiting from AI is autonomous navigation. Whether it's a self-driving car or a delivery drone, the robot must interpret sensor data to understand its surroundings, plan a route, and avoid obstacles. This process involves computer vision, sensor fusion, and machine learning to adapt to new or unexpected events, like a pedestrian stepping off the curb or a sudden obstacle on the road.

In the service industry, AI-powered robots are beginning to appear in restaurants, hotels, and retail settings. They can greet customers, deliver items, or assist with inventory management. Social robots equipped with natural language processing can interact with people more naturally, making them useful in healthcare settings as companions or aides.

One of the most exciting applications is in healthcare. Surgical robots already assist doctors in performing complex procedures with greater precision. AI-enhanced robotic systems can process real-time data from medical imaging devices, help guide surgical tools, and even learn from previous surgeries to refine techniques. This synergy of robotics and AI has the potential to make healthcare safer and more efficient.

Despite the promise, challenges remain. Robots need robust sensors and algorithms to safely operate in unpredictable environments. They also require significant energy, posing engineering and environmental constraints. Ethical concerns arise around job displacement, privacy, and the militarization of robots (e.g., autonomous drones or weapon systems). Regulation and responsible innovation are crucial to ensure that robotic AI is developed and deployed in beneficial ways.

As technology advances, robots will undoubtedly become more capable and more common in daily life. From assembly lines to city streets, these AI-powered machines can enhance productivity, improve safety, and potentially free humans from dangerous or mundane tasks, thus reshaping labor markets and social structures around the world.

9

Chapter 9: AI in Everyday Life

If you pause to think about it, you might be surprised at how frequently artificial intelligence already intersects with daily life. From unlocking your smartphone with facial recognition to receiving personalized recommendations on your favorite streaming service, AI quietly works behind the scenes to make technology more intuitive, efficient, and convenient.

Smartphones are one of the most common avenues for AI in everyday life. Voice assistants like Siri, Alexa, and Google Assistant use natural language processing to interpret your commands, whether you're asking for directions or dictating a text message. AI-driven keyboard apps can predict the words you're about to type, improving both speed and accuracy.

On social media platforms, recommendation algorithms analyze your engagement—what you like, comment on, or share—to tailor your feed to what the system believes you find most interesting. This personalization can enhance user experience by surfacing relevant content, but it also raises concerns about the creation of "filter bubbles," where users see only viewpoints similar to their own.

E-commerce sites like Amazon employ AI to suggest products you might like, based on your browsing and purchase history. Likewise, Netflix and YouTube use AI-driven recommendation engines to point you toward shows or videos you'll likely enjoy. While this personalization helps you discover new favorites, it also highlights how much of your data is collected to fuel these algorithms.

Banking and finance also leverage AI for everyday convenience. Fraud detection systems monitor transactions for unusual patterns, sending alerts if something suspicious is detected. Chatbots on bank websites can answer common questions or help you find information without waiting on hold for a human representative.

AI is also making inroads into home appliances, from thermostats that learn your temperature preferences to refrigerators that track groceries and suggest recipes. In smart homes, devices can communicate with each other, adjusting lights or playing music based on voice commands. While these conveniences are becoming more affordable, it's important to remember that connected devices also collect data, which could raise privacy issues if not properly safeguarded.

Transportation is another area where AI impacts daily life. Navigation apps analyze real-time traffic data to recommend the fastest route, while ride-sharing apps dynamically set fares and match drivers with riders. Autonomous vehicles remain a developing technology, but they already appear in pilot programs around the world, offering a glimpse into the future of safer, more efficient travel.

All these examples illustrate how AI is deeply woven into our routines. While most AI applications are designed to enhance convenience and efficiency, they also prompt important questions about data usage, privacy, and ethical responsibility in an increasingly connected world.

10

Chapter 10: The Societal Impact of AI

Artificial Intelligence is not just a technological achievement—it's a social one. Its influence extends beyond algorithms and data; it shapes how we work, communicate, and make decisions. As AI systems become more integrated into every facet of modern life, understanding their societal impact becomes essential.

One major impact is on **employment and labor markets**. AI-driven automation can handle repetitive or dangerous tasks, potentially improving safety and freeing human workers for more creative or complex roles. However, it can also displace jobs, especially those involving routine, predictable tasks. This displacement can lead to economic inequality if workers lack the training or resources to transition into new roles.

Education also feels the effects of AI. Personalized learning platforms can adjust the pace and difficulty of coursework to meet individual student needs, potentially closing learning gaps. Yet, reliance on AI-driven tools raises questions about data privacy and the potential for algorithmic bias in educational assessments.

In **healthcare**, AI's societal impact is largely positive, with innovations like early disease detection and efficient resource allocation. These systems can reduce physician workload and improve patient outcomes. However, issues arise around data security and the risk of AI making critical decisions without adequate human oversight.

Bias and fairness concerns loom large. AI models trained on skewed or incomplete datasets can perpetuate stereotypes or discriminate against certain groups. For instance, facial recognition systems have been criticized for performing poorly on individuals with darker skin tones, leading to misidentifications. Such biases can have real-world consequences, affecting everything from job screenings to law enforcement.

Another significant concern is **privacy**. Data is the lifeblood of AI, and modern AI systems often require massive amounts of personal information. Striking the right balance between technological advancement and individual privacy remains a challenge. Excessive data collection can lead to misuse or unintended leaks, eroding public trust in AI systems and companies that develop them.

Economic and global power dynamics are also shifting. Countries investing heavily in AI research and infrastructure may gain a competitive edge, potentially exacerbating global inequalities. At the same time, international collaboration on AI standards and ethics can foster a more equitable distribution of benefits.

In sum, AI has the power to transform society in both beneficial and concerning ways. Its impact is rarely neutral, reflecting choices made by developers, policymakers, and businesses. Recognizing AI's societal ramifications helps us address the challenges it brings, ensuring that the technology serves the common good rather than deepening existing inequities.

11

Chapter 11: AI Ethics and Responsibility

As AI systems become more ingrained in society, questions of ethics and responsibility take center stage. The power of AI to automate decisions that can shape individual lives, influence public opinion, or even lead to life-and-death outcomes calls for clear ethical guidelines and accountability.

One of the primary ethical dilemmas arises from **algorithmic bias**. Machine learning models trained on biased data can perpetuate and even amplify societal inequities. For example, a recruitment algorithm trained primarily on male candidates might learn to favor male applicants, disadvantaging qualified women. In law enforcement, facial recognition systems have been criticized for higher error rates among certain ethnic groups. Awareness of such biases drives the need for auditing AI systems, diversifying training datasets, and involving ethicists, social scientists, and community stakeholders in the development process.

Another major concern is **transparency and explainability**.

Many AI models, particularly deep learning systems, operate as "black boxes," meaning their internal decision-making processes are not easily understood by humans. This opacity poses challenges in fields like healthcare, finance, or criminal justice, where decisions have ethical and legal ramifications. A lack of transparency can erode trust and make it difficult to rectify mistakes or biases. Researchers are actively working on methods for explainable AI that provide clearer insights into how these models arrive at their conclusions.

The question of **autonomy vs. human control** also emerges. How much authority should be delegated to AI systems, especially in high-stakes scenarios like military drones or autonomous vehicles? Striking the right balance between human oversight and technological automation is critical for preventing abuses and errors. In healthcare, for instance, AI can assist in diagnosis and treatment recommendations, but final decisions are best left to qualified medical professionals.

Privacy is another facet of AI ethics. Personal data fuels AI algorithms, but data collection and processing practices often lack adequate transparency and consent. People may not fully understand how their data is used, raising concerns about surveillance, data breaches, and the potential for misuse by corporations or governments.

Finally, there is the broader issue of **societal impact**. AI-driven automation may disrupt labor markets, influencing how wealth is distributed and potentially exacerbating inequality. Policymakers are exploring measures like universal basic income, job retraining programs, or tax incentives to mitigate these effects.

Ethical AI frameworks often call for inclusive and equitable design processes, ensuring technology benefits everyone, not just a select few.

In essence, building ethical AI requires more than technical expertise. It demands multidisciplinary collaboration, robust regulatory frameworks, and an ongoing commitment to fairness, transparency, and accountability—principles that help safeguard human dignity and societal well-being as AI continues to evolve.

12

Chapter 12: Bias and Fairness in AI

Bias in AI is not just an abstract concept—it has real-world consequences that can affect everything from job prospects to healthcare quality. AI systems learn patterns from data, and if that data contains historical or societal biases, the systems can reproduce and even magnify them. Understanding where bias comes from and how to address it is essential for creating fair and equitable AI technologies.

One common source of bias is **training data**. If the dataset used to train an AI model underrepresents certain groups, the model may perform poorly for those groups. For example, an image recognition system might misidentify individuals with darker skin if it was primarily trained on images of lighter-skinned people. Similarly, a language model could display gender stereotypes if it was trained on text that heavily associates certain professions with one gender.

Another issue is **labeling bias**, where the way data is annotated or categorized reflects subjective judgments. This can happen if the people labeling the data hold certain biases, consciously or unconsciously. Over time, these biases become entrenched in AI systems and go unnoticed until they cause harm.

Algorithmic bias can also arise from the design of the model itself. Certain optimization objectives or performance metrics might prioritize efficiency or overall accuracy, neglecting minority groups' specific needs. In such cases, the AI performs well for the majority but fails for smaller segments of the population, perpetuating inequality.

Addressing bias requires a multi-pronged approach. **Data audits** can uncover imbalances or skewed representations within training sets. Once identified, techniques like oversampling underrepresented groups or generating synthetic data can help create a more balanced dataset. **Algorithmic transparency** is another crucial aspect; developers need to understand why their models make certain decisions to detect hidden biases. They can use techniques such as local interpretable model-agnostic explanations (LIME) or Shapley values to gain insights into a model's inner workings.

Fairness metrics are also being developed. These metrics aim to quantify how equitably an AI system treats different groups. They include definitions like demographic parity, equalized odds, and predictive parity, each capturing different notions of fairness. However, no single metric can address all concerns simultaneously, so developers often face trade-offs.

Addressing bias isn't just a technical challenge; it's also a social one. Inclusive teams that reflect diverse perspectives are more likely to catch biases early. Regulation and standards can enforce fairness guidelines, ensuring companies take proactive steps to mitigate harmful outcomes. Ultimately, eliminating bias and ensuring fairness in AI is an ongoing process—one that demands continual vigilance, accountability, and collaboration across technical, legal, and societal domains.

13

Chapter 13: AI in Healthcare

Healthcare is a sector where artificial intelligence promises to make a profound impact. From diagnosing diseases at earlier stages to personalizing treatment plans, AI-driven tools offer the potential for more accurate, efficient, and inclusive medical care. While these advancements show great promise, they also introduce new ethical, privacy, and regulatory considerations.

One prominent application is **medical imaging analysis**. Radiologists spend countless hours examining X-rays, MRIs, and CT scans to detect anomalies like tumors or fractures. AI models trained on massive image datasets can assist by flagging suspicious areas that warrant a closer look. Some systems have even achieved near-human accuracy in detecting early signs of conditions like lung cancer or diabetic retinopathy. The result is faster diagnoses and potentially improved patient outcomes.

Predictive analytics is another area where AI excels. Hospitals and clinics collect vast amounts of patient data, including medical histories, lab results, and even data from wearable devices. Machine learning algorithms can sift through this data to predict which patients are at higher risk for complications, hospital readmissions, or chronic diseases. This information helps healthcare providers allocate resources more effectively and intervene earlier, potentially preventing serious health issues down the line.

Another transformative application is **personalized medicine**. By analyzing genetic information alongside lifestyle and environmental factors, AI can help tailor treatments to an individual's unique profile. This approach is already making strides in oncology, where doctors can customize chemotherapy regimens based on genetic markers associated with specific cancer types.

Despite these advantages, several challenges remain. **Data privacy** is a major concern. Medical records are highly sensitive, and AI algorithms need access to large volumes of data to function effectively. Ensuring that patient information is securely stored and ethically used is crucial. Additionally, healthcare professionals need to trust AI-driven recommendations, which means the AI must offer clear explanations and a proven track record of safety and efficacy.

Regulation is also evolving. Medical devices and software, including AI-based diagnostic tools, must meet rigorous standards before being approved for clinical use. Oversight bodies like the U.S. Food and Drug Administration (FDA) are developing guidelines to handle AI's dynamic nature, as these systems often learn and update themselves post-deployment.

Finally, AI should be viewed as a complement to, not a replace-

37

ment for, healthcare professionals. Empathy, clinical judgment, and patient-doctor relationships remain integral to quality care. When integrated thoughtfully, AI can augment medical expertise, streamline workflows, and ultimately enhance patient outcomes. By balancing innovation with ethical responsibility and patient-centric design, AI has the potential to revolutionize healthcare in profound, life-saving ways.

14

Chapter 14: AI in Education

Education is at the forefront of society's development, and AI has the potential to revolutionize how we teach and learn. By personalizing instruction and automating administrative tasks, AI can allow educators to focus more on what truly matters— guiding and mentoring students.

One of the most prominent uses of AI in education is **adaptive learning platforms**. These systems continually assess a student's understanding of a subject and adjust lesson material or difficulty levels accordingly. For example, if a student struggles with algebraic fractions, the platform can provide additional practice problems and explanatory videos. Conversely, if a student excels in a topic, the system advances them to more challenging material. This individualized approach ensures that students neither languish in boredom nor become overwhelmed.

Another area of innovation is **automated grading**, especially for multiple-choice and short-answer questions. AI can quickly and accurately score tests, providing immediate feedback to students and freeing teachers from routine grading tasks. More advanced AI tools are being developed to assess essays and written assignments, offering suggestions for improving grammar, structure, and even critical thinking. While these tools are not yet flawless, they show promise in aiding educators, especially in large classes where giving personalized feedback to each student is time-consuming.

Chatbots and virtual assistants can serve as supplementary tutors, available around the clock to answer students' queries. This instant access to help can bolster learning outside traditional classroom hours. In language learning, AI-driven apps track a learner's progress and adapt exercises in real-time. Speech recognition allows for advanced pronunciation feedback, making language acquisition more interactive and engaging.

However, AI in education also has potential pitfalls. **Data privacy** is a major concern, as these systems often collect detailed information about a student's performance, habits, and behaviors. Safeguarding this data is critical to protecting students' rights and well-being. There is also a risk of over-reliance on technology. While adaptive platforms are powerful, they should complement, not replace, human teachers, who provide emotional support, motivation, and critical thinking guidance that machines currently cannot replicate.

Another challenge is **algorithmic bias**. If a system is trained on data that reflects certain cultural or gender biases, it may inadvertently disadvantage some students by providing them with different levels of encouragement or difficulty. Ensuring that AI-driven educational tools are equitable and accessible is essential for creating an inclusive learning environment.

When used judiciously, AI can enrich the educational experience by personalizing learning, automating tedious tasks, and enhancing engagement. The key lies in integrating these tools responsibly, ensuring that the role of human educators remains central while leveraging AI's strengths to foster more effective, equitable, and inspiring learning experiences.

15

Chapter 15: AI in Business and Finance

Businesses and financial institutions were among the earliest adopters of AI technologies, capitalizing on machine learning and data analytics to streamline operations, reduce costs, and uncover new revenue streams. Whether it's predicting stock prices, personalizing customer experiences, or mitigating fraud, AI has become an invaluable tool in the corporate world.

Customer relationship management (CRM) platforms leverage AI to analyze customer interactions, segment audiences, and predict purchasing behaviors. This helps companies personalize marketing campaigns and product recommendations, increasing the likelihood of a sale. Chatbots also provide 24/7 customer support, handling routine inquiries and freeing human agents to tackle more complex issues.

In the realm of **finance**, AI-driven algorithms enable automated trading and investment strategies. These systems ingest massive amounts of market data—from historical stock prices to real-time news—and use machine learning techniques to identify patterns or anomalies. High-frequency trading firms rely on these algorithms to make rapid decisions, executing trades in fractions of a second. While this can improve market liquidity and efficiency, it also raises concerns about market manipulation and systemic risk if algorithms malfunction.

Fraud detection is another area where AI shines. Financial institutions use machine learning models to monitor transactions for suspicious patterns. For instance, if a credit card is suddenly used on another continent for large purchases, the system flags it for review or automatic blocking. Similarly, in insurance, AI can detect fraudulent claims by spotting inconsistencies in reported information.

Risk assessment benefits significantly from AI. Banks evaluate the creditworthiness of loan applicants by analyzing a range of data points, from credit scores to online footprints. Insurers calculate premiums based on predictions of claim probabilities, identifying high-risk profiles with greater precision. While these processes can be more accurate than traditional methods, they also heighten concerns about privacy and bias. If an AI model uses data proxies that correlate with race or socioeconomic status, it could inadvertently discriminate against certain groups.

The **supply chain** and **logistics** sectors also leverage AI for demand forecasting, route optimization, and inventory management. By predicting demand more accurately, companies can reduce waste, cut costs, and ensure that products are available when and where customers need them. Automated warehouses equipped with robotic systems can further streamline logistics, improving speed and accuracy.

Overall, AI is reshaping the business and finance sectors by increasing efficiency, refining decision-making, and unlocking novel forms of value creation. Yet, these gains must be balanced with ethical and regulatory considerations. Issues like data privacy, algorithmic bias, and accountability for automated decisions remain hot-button topics that firms must navigate to maintain trust and long-term sustainability in an AI-driven marketplace.

16

Chapter 16: The Future of Work and AI

The prospect of machines and algorithms taking over human jobs has long been a subject of speculation and anxiety. With the rapid advances in AI, especially in automation and machine learning, these concerns have intensified. However, the future of work in an AI-driven world may not be as straightforward as human vs. machine. Instead, it's more likely to involve a complex interplay where some roles become automated, others evolve, and entirely new ones emerge.

AI is particularly adept at handling **routine, repetitive tasks**—for instance, data entry, simple bookkeeping, or basic customer service queries. Automating these functions can free up human workers to focus on tasks requiring creativity, problem-solving, and emotional intelligence. This shift can potentially enhance productivity and job satisfaction, but it also demands significant workforce retraining to help displaced workers transition into new roles.

In **manufacturing**, robotics powered by AI can handle assembly line tasks with precision and speed. Advanced robots can adapt to changing conditions, reducing the need for frequent reprogramming. While this may reduce the number of low-skill jobs, it may also create demand for specialized technicians, engineers, and robotics experts.

Knowledge work is also affected. AI can analyze large datasets, generate reports, and even draft articles, challenging the notion that creative or analytical roles are immune to automation. Yet, human oversight remains crucial for interpreting results, ensuring quality, and providing nuanced judgment. Roles that combine human intuition with AI-driven insights—such as data scientists, AI ethicists, and strategic analysts—are on the rise.

Healthcare and **education** offer examples of how AI can augment human professionals rather than replace them. AI can handle administrative tasks, assist in diagnoses, or personalize learning, allowing doctors and teachers to devote more time to patient care and student engagement. This augmentation model suggests that in many fields, AI serves as a tool that complements rather than supplants human expertise.

The key to navigating the future of work lies in **education and retraining**. Workers need opportunities to develop new skills tailored to an AI-centric economy. Governments, educational institutions, and businesses must collaborate to create programs that help people transition to AI-enhanced roles. Furthermore, social safety nets or new policies may be necessary to mitigate potential inequalities that can arise from rapid automation.

Ultimately, AI's impact on the workforce will depend on how societies choose to implement and regulate these technologies. While automation poses challenges, it also opens doors to new opportunities and job categories, emphasizing the adaptability of the human workforce and the importance of informed, ethical adoption of AI in the workplace.

17

Chapter 17: Government, Policy, and AI

As AI increasingly influences many aspects of daily life—
from how we work to how we make healthcare decisions—
governments play a critical role in shaping the rules and
frameworks that guide AI's development and deployment.
Policy decisions about AI can affect everything from individual
privacy rights to international competitiveness.

One of the most pressing issues is **regulation**. Because AI can
impact public safety, fairness, and civil liberties, many argue
that it should be subject to oversight similar to other potentially harmful technologies or sectors (e.g., pharmaceuticals or
financial services). Policymakers face the challenge of crafting
rules that protect citizens without stifling innovation. Overly
restrictive laws could hamper research and economic growth,
while insufficient regulation might lead to harm or misuse.

Data protection laws have become increasingly relevant. Leg-
islation like the European Union's General Data Protection
Regulation (GDPR) establish guidelines on how personal data

can be collected, stored, and used. These frameworks often directly affect AI systems that rely on large datasets for training. Developers need to ensure their AI applications comply with consent, data minimization, and transparency requirements. Other regions are drafting or refining their own data protection regulations, creating a patchwork of rules that companies must navigate.

Ethical AI guidelines are also emerging, sponsored by governments and international organizations. These guidelines typically address issues like bias, transparency, accountability, and inclusivity. They aim to ensure that AI benefits society at large, rather than exacerbating existing inequalities. Some governments are also setting up dedicated agencies or task forces to keep pace with AI research and oversee its ethical implications.

Another key area is **economic policy**. Governments recognize the competitive advantage that comes from being a leader in AI research and infrastructure. Consequently, many nations are investing heavily in AI-focused education, public-private research partnerships, and the development of computing resources. These investments aim to foster local innovation and attract global talent. However, this race for AI leadership can also fuel international tensions, as countries vie for dominance in both commercial and military AI applications.

Military applications of AI raise ethical and geopolitical concerns. Autonomous weapons systems, surveillance technologies, and cyberwarfare capabilities can drastically alter the global security landscape. Some voices call for international treaties or agreements to regulate AI in warfare, akin to nuclear non-proliferation treaties.

Ultimately, the role of government in AI is to balance innovation with public interest, safeguarding human rights and welfare. Achieving this balance requires collaboration among policymakers, tech companies, researchers, and civil society. Ongoing dialogue and adaptive policy frameworks are essential, as the rapid pace of AI development demands continual reassessment of risks, benefits, and ethical considerations.

18

Chapter 18: AI and the Environment

As climate change and environmental degradation become increasingly urgent issues, AI has emerged as a powerful tool for understanding and addressing these challenges. Machine learning algorithms, computer vision, and predictive analytics offer new ways to monitor ecosystems, optimize resource use, and mitigate human impact on the planet.

One of the most promising applications is **climate modeling**. Scientists use AI to analyze vast amounts of historical climate data, weather patterns, and satellite imagery, generating more accurate simulations of future climate scenarios. These models help policymakers and researchers understand potential outcomes of global warming, such as sea-level rise or extreme weather events, enabling more informed decisions about infrastructure planning and disaster response.

Wildlife conservation also benefits from AI-driven innovations. Computer vision tools can process images from camera traps and aerial drones to track animal populations, identify poaching activities, and monitor habitat health. By automating data collection and analysis, conservationists gain real-time insights into at-risk species and can quickly intervene when they detect illegal activities.

In **agriculture**, AI can optimize the use of resources like water, fertilizers, and pesticides. Precision farming techniques employ sensors, satellite imagery, and machine learning to monitor crop health at a granular level. By targeting interventions precisely where they're needed, farmers reduce waste, save costs, and minimize environmental damage. Similar principles apply to fisheries and aquaculture, where AI can forecast fish populations and help maintain sustainable harvesting levels.

Another critical area is **energy management**. Smart grids equipped with AI can dynamically match energy supply with demand, reducing waste and lowering costs. Predictive maintenance algorithms can monitor wind turbines, solar panels, and other infrastructure, identifying potential failures before they become costly repairs or cause downtime. Moreover, AI can help buildings optimize heating, cooling, and lighting based on occupancy and weather conditions, significantly cutting energy consumption.

However, the use of AI for environmental purposes is not without downsides. Large AI models require substantial computational resources, leading to a **carbon footprint** from data centers powered by fossil fuels. Efforts are underway to make these centers more energy-efficient and to power them with renewable energy, but it remains a balancing act between AI's potential benefits and its environmental impact.

Finally, data collection initiatives must respect **privacy and ethical standards**, especially when drones or remote sensors capture information that could also reveal personal or sensitive details about people in the monitored areas. Despite these challenges, AI's role in environmental protection holds immense promise. By intelligently analyzing complex data and offering predictive insights, AI can help societies move toward more sustainable practices and mitigate some of the most pressing ecological threats of our time.

19

Chapter 19: The Future of AI

Predicting the future of AI is both exciting and fraught with uncertainty. The rapid progress made in areas like deep learning, natural language processing, and reinforcement learning suggests that AI will continue to evolve, shaping nearly every sector of society. Yet the path forward is not linear, and challenges remain.

One vision of the future involves the pursuit of **Artificial General Intelligence (AGI)**—systems with the flexibility and breadth of understanding comparable to human intelligence. While current AI systems excel at specific tasks, they lack the versatility to handle the wide range of activities that humans can. Achieving AGI would require significant breakthroughs in areas like transfer learning, common sense reasoning, and self-awareness. Some experts believe it may happen within this century, while others remain skeptical or warn about the dangers of creating AI that could surpass human intelligence.

In the near term, we're likely to see continued **automation** of tasks in sectors ranging from manufacturing to services. This will necessitate a shift in job roles and skill sets, fueling demand for professionals who can develop, manage, or collaborate with AI systems. AI will also become more embedded in daily life, from augmented reality applications to more intuitive home automation solutions.

Human-AI collaboration will be a key theme. Far from replacing human ingenuity, future AI tools could augment our capabilities, helping us solve complex problems in medicine, law, or environmental science. Advanced generative models might become creative partners in fields like art, design, and storytelling, prompting new forms of human-machine co-creation.

Ethical and regulatory frameworks will also evolve. As AI's influence grows, so does the need to ensure fairness, accountability, and transparency. Researchers and policymakers will continue working on ways to detect and mitigate bias, manage privacy risks, and maintain human oversight over critical decisions. We can expect more formalized standards, certifications, and perhaps even licensing requirements for AI systems that impact public welfare.

International cooperation could shape the trajectory of AI. If nations collaborate on setting universal standards and ethical guidelines, they can minimize conflict and harness AI to tackle global issues like climate change or pandemics. Conversely, if AI becomes a domain of intense geopolitical rivalry, it could exacerbate tensions and lead to an arms race in lethal autonomous weapons or surveillance technologies.

Ultimately, the future of AI will be shaped by the interplay of technological advancements, economic incentives, social values, and political choices. Whether AI becomes a tool that primarily benefits humanity or a technology that deepens inequities depends largely on the collective actions of governments, businesses, researchers, and ordinary citizens in the years to come.

20

Chapter 20: Conclusion and Next Steps

Throughout this book, we've seen how artificial intelligence has evolved from a speculative concept into a transformative force reshaping our workplaces, schools, homes, and even our understanding of what it means to be human. AI touches nearly every corner of modern life, offering remarkable benefits—efficiency, personalization, insights—and equally formidable challenges, such as bias, privacy concerns, and ethical dilemmas.

A clear takeaway is that AI is not a monolith; it's an umbrella term for a spectrum of technologies—machine learning, deep learning, natural language processing, computer vision, and more. Each branch has unique applications, benefits, and risks. Understanding these nuances can help demystify AI and allow us to engage with it responsibly and creatively.

Equally important is recognizing that AI's impact is shaped by humans. The data we choose to collect, the objectives we set for algorithms, and the regulations (or lack thereof) we put in place all influence how AI serves society. If we feed biased or incomplete datasets into AI systems, we amplify existing inequalities. Conversely, if we carefully audit data and include diverse perspectives in development teams, AI can become more equitable and inclusive.

As you move forward, here are some next steps you might consider:

1. **Stay Informed**: AI technology evolves rapidly. Keeping up with reputable sources—news outlets, academic journals, and thought leaders—can help you understand new developments and their broader implications.

2. **Engage in Dialogue**: Public debate and policy discussions around AI are ongoing, and your voice matters. Whether through community forums or online platforms, discussing AI's impact on jobs, ethics, or education fosters a more informed public discourse.

3. **Acquire Digital Literacy**: You don't need to become a machine learning engineer to benefit from or critically assess AI. Basic understanding of data science and computational thinking can empower you to use AI tools effectively and responsibly.

4. **Advocate for Responsible AI**: As a consumer, voter, or professional, you can push for ethical standards, transparency, and accountability in AI systems. This might involve supporting regulations that protect data privacy or challenging businesses to audit their algorithms for fairness.

5. **Explore Opportunities**: AI is creating new roles and opportunities in almost every sector. From healthcare to finance, environmental science to entertainment, exploring how AI

intersects with your field can open doors for innovation.

AI is neither a magic bullet nor an inevitable doom—it's a toolkit created by people, for people. Its trajectory will be defined by how we choose to deploy it, govern it, and integrate it into our daily lives. By understanding its capabilities and limitations, we can harness AI's power for societal good while remaining vigilant against potential harms. The future of AI is still unwritten, and each of us has a role to play in shaping it.

21

References

1. Russell, S. J., & Norvig, P. (2020). *Artificial Intelligence: A Modern Approach* (4th Edition). Pearson.
2. Goodfellow, I., Bengio, Y., & Courville, A. (2016). *Deep Learning*. MIT Press.
3. Turing, A. M. (1950). "Computing Machinery and Intelligence." *Mind*, 59(236), 433–460.
4. McCarthy, J. et al. (1955). "A Proposal for the Dartmouth Summer Research Project on Artificial Intelligence."
5. LeCun, Y., Bengio, Y., & Hinton, G. (2015). "Deep Learning." *Nature*, 521(7553), 436–444.
6. European Commission. (2020). *White Paper on Artificial Intelligence: a European approach to excellence and trust.*
7. DeepMind. (2016). "AlphaGo." https://deepmind.com/research/alphago
8. IBM Research. (1997). "Deep Blue." https://www.ibm.com/ibm/history/ibm100/us/en/icons/deepblue/
9. U.S. Food & Drug Administration. (2021). *Artificial Intelligence and Machine Learning (AI/ML)-Enabled Medical*

Devices.

10. United Nations. (2021). *AI for Good Global Summit.* https://a iforgood.itu.int/

End of Book